THE CLOUD RIDER

TINA SHAW

Published by Pearson Education Limited, Edinburgh Gate, Harlow, Essex, CM20 2JE
Registered company number: 872828

www.pearsonschools.co.uk

First published by Pearson
a division of Pearson New Zealand Ltd
67 Apollo Drive, Rosedale, North Shore 0632, New Zealand
Associated companies throughout the world

Text © Pearson 2011

Page Layout: Ruby-Anne Fenning
Cover Design and Illustrations: Sara Bellamy

The right of Tina Shaw to be identified as author of this work has been asserted by
her in accordance with the Copyright, Designs and Patents Act 1988.

First published 2011
This edition published 2012

2023
16

British Library Cataloguing in Publication Data
A catalogue record for this book is available from the British Library

ISBN 978-0-43507-585-9

Printed in Great Britain by Ashford Colour Press Ltd.

Acknowledgements
We would like to thank the children and teachers of Bangor Central Integrated
Primary School, NI; Bishop Henderson C of E Primary School, Somerset; Brookside
Community Primary School, Somerset; Cheddington Combined School,
Buckinghamshire; Cofton Primary School, Birmingham; Dair House Independent
School, Buckinghamshire; Deal Parochial School, Kent; Lawthorn Primary School,
North Ayrshire; Newbold Riverside Primary School, Rugby and Windmill Primary
School, Oxford for their invaluable help in the development and trialling of the Bug
Club resources.

Every effort has been made to contact copyright holders of material reproduced in
this book. Any omissions will be rectified in subsequent printings if notice is given
to the publishers.

A division of Pearson New Zealand Ltd

CONTENTS

Chapter 1

CHASE IN THE CLOUDS

"Got you!" cried Jay, tagging Ellie's back.

Ellie just laughed and started chasing him. They were playing "tag" on the top field. It was better with more people, but their best friends had gone away for the holidays. Not that it really mattered. Being twins, Jay and Ellie always had each other.

Ellie cornered her brother near the Peak, tagging his back.

"Hey, that's not fair," panted Jay.

Ellie stopped to catch her breath, then looked out over the field. The twins loved this field, because it was the highest point of their farm. You could see a long way in every direction. Especially if you climbed up the Peak – a lumpy hill that reached for the sky.

The grass up here was really long now. Their father used to run sheep on the top field, but he hadn't done that for ages. He said the weather was too unpredictable. They used to have long, warm summers and dry winters.

Lately, it always seemed to be raining or stormy. It was better if the sheep were kept in the fields closer to home, Dad said.

"Race you to the Peak," shouted Jay.

Ellie looked at the jagged top. It was wrapped in dark, low cloud. "I'm not going up there. It's going to rain."

"Don't be such a wimp!"

"I'm not," called Ellie, walking away. She was heading for the track through the trees. Back at the house, Mum would have the fire going in the kitchen. It would be warm and cosy.

"Hey!" shouted Jay. "Look at that!"

"You can't fool me that easily," said Ellie, over her shoulder. Jay was always getting her to look at something, but it was usually just a trick.

"Ellie, true," called Jay. "You've got to see!"

She stopped walking and put her hands on her hips. When she turned, Jay was staring up at the sky. But Ellie was not going to be fooled this time. She marched back to where Jay was standing and tickled him under the chin.

"Quit it," he grumbled. "Look!" He pointed at the sky.

Ellie couldn't help it – she looked. Then she gasped. Flashes of light were sparking in the thick, dark clouds. It looked like lightning, except the flashes were red. They should get back. With all the bad weather lately, Dad had warned them not to stay outside during storms.

"We've got to get under cover!" Ellie cried.

The twins knew all about lightning. Sometimes it struck one of the sheep. Their mother had told them they must run for cover if they were outside during a lightning storm. They weren't to shelter in the trees they used for firewood though. That would be dangerous.

Jay wasn't moving. He was still staring at the sky. "What's that?" he asked.

Flashing through the clouds was a thing that looked like a huge bird. It was as pale as sheep's wool and had long arms and legs.

The twins watched as the strange creature raced towards the Peak and vanished into the thick cloud. They were dumbfounded.

"What was it?" gasped Ellie.

"I ... I don't know," whispered Jay. "Could it be a really big hawk?"

"No way. Hawks are brown. That thing was –"

Three red streaks zoomed past above them, heading for the Peak.

"Oh, look!" cried Ellie.

Clashing sounds came from the Peak – like the sound two saucepans make when they're banged together.

Suddenly, with a shriek, the first creature flew out of the cloud. It raced across the sky.

The twins stared at each other. They couldn't believe their eyes.

"What's happening?" said Ellie. She wanted to run for home.

"Those red things are chasing the bird," said Jay.

"We should get Dad," said Ellie, trying to be sensible.

"I want to keep watching," said Jay, with big eyes. "Besides, they might be gone by the time we get back."

"But what are they?" asked Ellie, frowning.

The three red shapes raced after their prey, moving much faster than sheepdogs. As they dived and twirled, sparks flew off them. Shrieks sounded in the air.

"They're going to catch it!" shouted Jay.

Ellie couldn't see where the pale creature had gone. "Where is it?" she wondered aloud. "Maybe it's got away."

Just then, bursting out of thick cloud, there it was – the bird-like creature. And, right behind it, the three red shapes. There was a blast and a shriek.

"Oh!" cried Ellie. "They got it."

As they watched, the bird-like creature started to fall out of the sky. Slowly, it turned and twisted, as if trying to get back up to the clouds, but it kept falling. Down and down, towards the ground.

"It's going to crash!" shouted Jay.

However, at the last minute, the thing put out its arms – great, feathery arms – and drifted to the ground.

The twins ran over to it. The creature was as pale as summer cloud, almost see-through. Its eyes were closed.

"What is it?" whispered Ellie.

"I don't know," Jay whispered back.

The thing moaned and moved its head towards its shoulder. It was hurt.

Chapter 2

A Voice Like Smoke

The twins stood staring down at the creature. It was like something out of a fairy tale.

"A . . . are you all right?" asked Ellie.

Jay gave her a nudge. "Course it's not all right," he hissed.

"Well, what would you say? We don't even know if it can talk. What if it just makes noises like a horse or something?"

"Be quiet or you'll wake it up," Jay muttered.

"But I *want* it to wake up. Maybe we can help it."

"We can't help something when we don't even know what it is."

"So what? It's hurt. We've still got to try."

There was a movement in the grass. While they were arguing, the twins had almost forgotten about the creature lying at their feet. Now it was looking up at them with eyes the colour of water. Jay and Ellie stared back. They had never seen anything so strange.

Then the creature started to speak in a voice like smoke. "Human children," it said, as if trying out the words. It had probably never spoken to people before. "You ask what I am. I am a Cloud Rider."

"A *what*?" blurted Jay.

Ellie sank to her knees beside the creature. "You can understand us?"

The Cloud Rider nodded.

"What were those things chasing you?" asked Jay.

The Cloud Rider looked up at the sky. There was no sign of the red streaks now, but the creature still looked worried. "They are called Werrets," it murmured.

The twins glanced at each other in wonder. "But why are they chasing you?" asked Jay.

"Because the Werrets . . ." the creature started to say. Then it began to cough, and a thin dribble of liquid came out of its mouth.

"Oh!" cried Ellie. "How can we help you?"

The Cloud Rider's gaze went to her

anxious face. "Take me to shelter. Before the Werrets return."

"We need somewhere to hide him," said Ellie, looking back up at Jay. "But where?"

Jay frowned, thinking. Sometimes they played in a cave hidden in the trees. Once they had even camped there overnight with Dad. "How about the cave?" he suggested.

"Yes, good idea." Ellie turned back to the creature. "Can you, um, walk?"

The creature didn't seem to know what she meant. Then he told the twins that they should carry him. "You will find me very light."

Gently, they lifted him up – Ellie's hands under his shoulders, Jay holding his legs. The Cloud Rider was as light as a bird.

As quickly as they could, they carried him across the field, heading towards the trees. Ellie kept looking over her shoulder, worried that the Werrets might be coming after them. But the field was empty.

There was a track through the trees to the cave, and it didn't take long to get there. The entrance was partly hidden by ferns. Carefully, the twins pushed them aside. Inside the cave, they laid the Cloud Rider on the soft, dry earth.

Ellie went to find some moss. Then she put it under the creature's head, hoping to make him more comfortable.

"We'll need a blanket," she said. "It'll be cold."

Jay wasn't so sure. "It'll be colder up there, in the clouds. It's probably much warmer for him in here."

The children sat on either side of the creature, wondering what to do next. They watched his thin chest move up and down as he breathed. He was covered all over with long, wispy feathers.

The Cloud Rider

Ellie had never seen feathers like them before. They weren't strong, like a blackbird's feathers. And they weren't shiny like a chicken's either.

The creature groaned.

"We should put something under his shoulder," said Jay.

"I'll get some more moss," said Ellie, hurrying out of the cave.

Outside, the sky was getting darker and darker. It was starting to get late, and the rain couldn't be far away. The twins knew they would have to go home, but how could they leave the Cloud Rider alone?

Gently, Jay held up the creature's shoulder as Ellie packed the moss underneath. "We have to go home," he told the Cloud Rider. "We're on holiday, so we can come back first thing in the morning."

"That's right," said Ellie, nodding. "And we can bring some things for you."

The twins stood up.

"We'll be back soon, Cloud Rider," said Jay.

At first they couldn't tell if he had heard them or not, but then the creature opened his eyes and gazed up at them. He seemed to understand. Then he closed his eyes again and they left.

The twins ran through the trees, then hurried down towards the lower fields and the farmhouse.

At the stile, Ellie stopped and looked at Jay. "What if . . ." she began. She was thinking about a thrush they had once rescued from the cat. She had put it in a shoebox, in a nest of paper, but in the morning, when they went to check on the little bird, it was dead.

Being twins, Jay usually knew what Ellie was thinking, even if she didn't say it out loud. "He'll be all right," he said. "You wait and see."

Jay took off across the paddock towards the house. Ellie followed more slowly. The lights were already shining in the farmhouse and smoke was curling from the chimney.

Chapter 3

SOMETHING ODD

"Finally, there you are!" said their mother. She was at the bench, cutting up carrots for soup. "Thought we'd have to send out a search party," she added, smiling.

Ellie flopped into a chair in front of the fire and warmed her hands. Jay went to see if there were any cookies left in the tin.

"Mum," said Ellie, "we found something funny in the top field."

"Funny ha-ha or funny odd?" asked Mum.

"Something *odd*," said Jay, sitting at the big kitchen table.

"Who's found something odd?" asked their father, coming in through the back door. He was still wearing his wellies and was carrying a young lamb.

"Mark!" cried their mother. "Take off those dirty boots!"

"Not till I've put this lamb down," he said, winking at Ellie. "Jay, run and fetch the dog's old basket, will you?"

When Jay came back with the wicker

basket – too small now for Fluff, the family pet – Dad gently laid the lamb in it. He put the basket in front of the fire.

"It's so tiny," said Ellie, stroking the lamb's soft ear.

"Its mother fell down the hillside," said Dad. "But I found the lamb up the top on the grass. So here it is."

"Is it all right?" asked Jay, frowning. The lamb looked awfully weak and its eyes were dull.

"I don't know," said their father, taking off his cap. "It's been raining and it might have got a chill."

Ellie knew that such a young lamb could get sick very easily. She hoped it would make it through the day.

"Boots," said Mum firmly, pointing at their father's feet.

Dad winked at Ellie again and went out the door to take off his wellies.

"Mum," said Ellie, "shall I fetch the bottle?"

"Yes, please, Ellie. And, Jay, you can get out the tin of formula."

The twins had looked after young lambs before and they knew what to do. Together, they mixed the special milk formula in a plastic baby's bottle. They boiled the kettle, poured some hot water into a bowl, and put the bottle in the water to heat.

"Maybe the Cloud Rider would like some milk, too," said Ellie, her voice low.

Jay shrugged. "He's not a lamb."

"Yes, but we have to take him something to eat," insisted Ellie.

"What are you two whispering about?" asked their mother.

"We found a Cloud Rider," Jay told her.

"You found a *what*?" asked a laughing voice. It was their older brother, Peter, taking his boots off at the back door.

"A Cloud Rider," said Ellie.

Jay kicked her ankle to tell her to be quiet. Peter was always teasing them.

"And what's that, then?" asked Peter, sitting down at the table.

Ellie told him what had happened in the top field.

"Well, well!" said Peter. "Chased by Werrets – terrible things!"

"Peter," warned Mum, "don't tease the twins."

"Hey, I believe them," he said, laughing. "Just like the last time, when they said there was a purple cat in the vegetable garden."

"But there *was* a –" Ellie started to say, before Jay kicked her again.

"It was probably a big rat," said Peter. "Then there was that fairy in the rose bush."

Ellie blushed.

"Ellie was only four then," said Jay hotly.

Peter chuckled affectionately. "Mum," he said, "what's for dinner? I'm starving."

"We're having soup," said Mum.

Dad came back inside in his thick socks. He started talking to Peter about a fence he wanted to make along the side of the hill to stop any more sheep from falling down. Mum put out bread and butter and soup bowls.

"Go and wash your hands," she told the twins.

In the bathroom, Ellie and Jay jostled to get at the soap and water.

"You and your big mouth," hissed Jay.

"You told, too," said Ellie.

"But you shouldn't have told Peter," he said. Jay hated their brother's teasing.

"I don't care," said Ellie, flicking water into Jay's face. She ran back out to the kitchen.

Over dinner, Peter said to their father, "The twins found something up in the top field."

Dad looked up, interested. "Oh, yes? What was that?"

Ellie blushed again, wishing they hadn't

said anything. "A Cloud Rider."

"A what?" asked Dad.

"*You* know," said Peter, nudging his father with an elbow, "one of those things that fly around in the clouds."

"Now that's enough," said Mum, putting down her soup spoon. "You both know the twins have got big imaginations."

Peter hooted. "I'll say!"

Dad smiled. "There's nothing wrong with a bit of imagination."

"But we *didn't* imagine it," protested Jay. "It's true!"

"There really *is* a Cloud Rider," said Ellie firmly. "It's hurt and we put it in the cave where it would be safe."

Their mother shivered. "I hate that cave. It's full of spiders."

"Injured, eh?" said Dad, taking another piece of bread. "Well, you'd better look after it, like that lamb."

The talk turned next to the lamb, and the

family forgot about the Cloud Rider.

That night, Ellie and Jay took turns staying up to feed the lamb. It sucked hungrily at the teat on the bottle.

"I hope you'll be all right, little lamb," whispered Ellie.

Chapter 4
SOMETHING IMPORTANT TO DO

The next morning, Ellie woke up early, even though it wasn't a school day. For a moment, she lay there, warm and cosy in her bed, thinking she ought to get up. Wasn't there something important she had to do today? There was the lamb to look after, but Mum would be doing that now. She and Jay had set the alarm and got up every two hours through the night to feed it. Ellie was tired now and wanted to go back to sleep, but something else was niggling at her.

Then she remembered – the Cloud Rider!

Ellie jumped out of bed and ran to Jay's room to wake him – but his bed was empty. She felt a pang. What if he'd gone out without her? He might be up at the cave already.

Voices were coming from the kitchen, and Ellie ran down the hall towards them. Jay was sitting by the fire, looking sleepy and holding the baby's bottle while the lamb sucked at it. A pot of porridge was bubbling on the stove, and the windows were all fogged up.

"What are you doing?" asked Ellie, sitting in the other chair.

"What's it look like?" snapped Jay.

"But Mum can do that. We've got the Cloud Rider to look after."

Jay's eyes widened. "I thought that was just a dream!" He pulled the bottle out of the lamb's mouth with a pop.

Mum came bustling in. "Come on, you two, you'll catch a chill if you don't get out of your pyjamas."

She didn't have to say it twice. The twins hurried out of the kitchen.

Once they were in their warm clothes, Ellie and Jay quickly helped themselves to a bowl of porridge with brown sugar and milk. Their mother had gone out to help on the farm, so they had the kitchen to themselves.

"Do you think he'd like some of this porridge?" asked Jay, spooning up the last mouthful.

Ellie looked doubtful. "I don't know. He wouldn't see much porridge up in the sky."

They both giggled.

"Okay, so what do you think he eats?"

Ellie thought about a project her class had done about birds. They had drawn posters to show all the different foods a bird liked to eat. "Insects?" she suggested.

Jay frowned, thinking. "Um, what about nectar?"

"We could make some sugar water, like Mum puts out for the birds in winter."

"Okay," said Jay, jumping up.

They put their bowls in the sink. Ellie found an old drink bottle and filled it with warm water. Then Jay sprinkled half a spoonful of sugar from the sugar bowl into the water. That might be sweet enough for birds, he thought, but not for a large Cloud Rider. He added another spoonful of sugar. That didn't seem enough either, so he put in some more.

"What are you doing?" asked Mum, coming into the kitchen.

Jay jumped, spilling sugar all over the bench. "Nothing," he muttered.

"We're making up some food to take to the Cloud Rider," explained Ellie.

"Oh, right," said their mother, smiling. "While you're at it, you could make him some honey sandwiches. When you two were little, that's about all you lived on."

"He's not a kid," said Jay.

"No, but . . ." Mum looked at them for a moment, then shrugged her shoulders and went out again.

Ellie looked at her brother. "We *could* make some honey sandwiches. Even if the Cloud Rider doesn't eat them, *we* could."

"Okay," said Jay, fetching the loaf of bread.

While he was making the sandwiches, Ellie got a baby's bottle and started to mix up some of the lamb's formula.

"He won't like milk," scoffed Jay.

"You don't know that," said Ellie, carefully measuring out the formula.

"Bet you he won't."

"How much do you bet?"

"I bet you the dishes tonight," said Jay. Each night one of the twins had to help with the dishes and tonight it was Jay's turn.

"All right," said Ellie, "you're on."

When everything was ready, the twins packed it all into a basket and set off over the fields. In the distance, they could see their father and Peter working on the new fence along the hillside.

They climbed over the stile and walked across the fields. At the trees, the twins followed the path up the slope. Near the top, they turned off to the right, towards the cave.

All was quiet at the entrance to the cave.

"Do you think he's still there?" whispered Ellie, worried.

"Don't know," Jay whispered back.

They were both thinking the same thing – that the Cloud Rider had vanished during the night.

But, when they parted the ferns and went inside, there he was, still lying where they had left him. The creature opened his eyes when he heard the twins, and seemed to smile.

Chapter 5

ALL ALONE IN THE SKY

The twins sat cross-legged on the ground and watched as the Cloud Rider sat up carefully. It didn't look as if he was used to sitting or lying on something solid. He patted the ground with his feathery, claw-like hand.

"Sleeping is hard on this ground," he said, in his strange, smoky voice. "Do human children sleep on dirt?"

Jay chuckled. "No way. We have beds."

"What is beds?" asked the creature.

"Um, kind of like thick, fluffy clouds."

"What do *you* do when you want to sleep?" asked Ellie.

"I sleep in the clouds," he told them. "Always drifting."

"Don't you ever come down to Earth?" asked Jay.

"Sometimes," said the creature. "I like to walk on the grathe."

The twins exchanged a look. "Oh, you mean grass," guessed Ellie.

"Grass," agreed the Cloud Rider.

"But don't you get bored?" asked Jay, thinking how much he liked to watch television.

The creature gazed silently at him.

"I don't think he knows what you mean," said Ellie.

Jay unpacked the basket. He lined up the bottle of milk, the sugar water, an apple, the honey sandwiches and a choc-mint cookie (his favourite).

"We brought some food," he said.

The Cloud Rider looked at the things Jay had unpacked, but made no move to try anything.

Ellie picked up the bottle of milk. "This is milk," she explained. "It's like, um . . . It's what baby animals drink."

The Cloud Rider took the bottle between his bird-like claws and sniffed at it. Then he turned it upside down. A few drops of milk escaped from the baby bottle's rubber teat.

Ellie took it back and turned it up the right way. "You have to suck at it," she said.

Jay rolled his eyes. "He's not a lamb," he hissed.

Ellie ignored him. The Cloud Rider put the teat in his mouth and sucked. His eyes widened, then he spat a mouthful of milk onto the ground.

"See, I told you," said Jay, grinning. "He hates it."

Just then the creature tried the milk again and didn't seem to mind it after all. "Milk," he said, blinking. It was obvious he had never tasted milk before.

"Your turn to do the dishes tonight," said Ellie smugly.

Jay handed the Cloud Rider the sugar water next. That seemed to go down better. In fact, the creature drank half of it in one swallow.

Next, he tried one of

the honey sandwiches, but, instead of taking a bite, the Cloud Rider pulled apart the two slices of bread and licked off the honey.

"Hmmm, like pollen," he said.

Jay picked up the other sandwich and started to eat it. Ellie frowned at him, but he only said, "Don't want to waste it."

"Good," said the Cloud Rider. "I am feeling better now."

"Were you very hurt?" asked Ellie.

"Hurt a little," he said, shaking his head gently. "There is pain . . ." He moved his hand towards his shoulder. "And my wing is not working properly."

Ellie looked at the Cloud Rider's feathery arm. It did look a bit like a wing.

"What happened up there?" asked Jay.

The creature made a snorting noise. "Those Werrets, always they try to hurt me. It is their nature to be like that."

"But why?" asked Ellie.

"They want to frighten me away. Make me

go away from here."

"What are they?" asked Jay.

The creature blinked his silvery eyes. "They are like me, only dark. I want to keep the clouds in order, but the Werrets want only storms and bad weather. That is what they need."

"Why is that?" asked Jay.

"I am not sure," said the Cloud Rider. "It is something to do with gas, or warm air, coming up from the Earth. When there are heavy clouds, there is more warm air. The Werrets like this kind of air."

"Our father says the weather's been getting worse lately," said Ellie.

The Cloud Rider looked thoughtful. "Yes, that is true. Because there is only one of me and many Werrets. It is hard to keep order."

"So why don't you get some more Cloud Riders to help?" asked Jay.

"Where would they come from?" asked the creature, looking sad. The twins didn't know what to say to that. "For a long time," continued the Cloud Rider, "there has been only me here. And, if I leave this place to look for others of my kind, the Werrets will take over."

"Where are the other Cloud Riders?" asked Ellie.

"I do not know," he replied slowly. "There was a group of us. We got separated in a big storm." He bowed his head. "When I got free from the storm, I was alone."

The twins looked at each other. The Cloud Rider must be lonely without other creatures like him. It was hard for both Ellie and Jay to imagine being alone – they always had each other.

"But it does not matter. Even by myself, I must control the Werrets." The Cloud Rider took a shuddery breath. "Or you will always have bad weather here."

Ellie and Jay frowned at each other. That would be terrible. Their farm, and all the countryside around it, depended on good weather. It was hard to imagine not having sun or blue skies again.

The creature pointed at the cookie. "What is that?"

Ellie snorted. "It's Jay's favourite food."

The Cloud Rider licked the top of the cookie. His eyes widened in surprise. Then he stuffed it whole into his mouth and closed his eyes.

"What's that noise he's making?" Jay whispered.

"I think he's humming," said Ellie. As they watched, the Cloud Rider spat out a sticky glob of mint filling. He had sucked off all the chocolate.

Chapter 6
DAD'S SUGGESTION

Slowly, the twins made their way back to the farmhouse, thinking about the Cloud Rider and the Werrets. A flock of sheep scattered as they walked towards them.

"Those Werrets look scary," said Ellie.

"I'd give them a blast if I could," said Jay angrily.

Ellie knew what he meant. The Cloud Rider was so soft, like a lamb, and the Werrets were the worst kind of bullies. It was obvious the creature had to get back up to the clouds – and soon. They had to help him. But how? Maybe Mum would know, thought Ellie.

"At least he liked my cookie," said Jay smugly.

"He drank my milk, too," said Ellie.

"But not very much of it."

"Doesn't matter," she said. "You still have to do the dishes tonight."

At the garden gate, Fluff ran up to meet them. She was small and pretty and lived inside the house. Not like the sheepdogs, which lived outside in kennels.

The twins took off their wellies at the back door and went into the kitchen.

Dad was sitting with the lamb on his lap, feeding it.

"It's had nearly the whole bottle," he told them, sounding pleased. "It's doing really well, this little fella."

Ellie plopped down into the other chair. She patted the lamb's curly coat and thought about how much better the Cloud Rider had looked after drinking the sugar water. He was doing well, too.

"Where's Mum?" asked Ellie.

"She's gone into town to do some shopping," said Dad. "Why, what's up?"

"Oh, nothing."

"We've been up to see the Cloud Rider," blurted Jay.

Their father put the lamb back in the basket. "How's he getting on?" he asked seriously.

"Dad, the poor thing can't fly properly. And he's got to get back up in the sky," cried Ellie, "or the Werrets will take over."

"And we'll get lots more bad weather," added Jay.

"That'd be no good," said their father, his eyes twinkling. "We need the good weather for the lambs."

"That's right," agreed Jay.

"But we don't know how to help him," said Ellie.

"That's tricky." Dad scratched his head. "Well, when I was your age and had a problem to solve, you know what I used to do?"

"No, what?" the twins both asked at the same time.

"I'd go and see Old Tanty," he told them with a wink.

"But Old Tanty's, like, a hundred," said Jay in horror.

"She's not that old, son," said Dad, laughing. "And she hasn't always been old, you know. When I was a kid, she was just like your mum."

Ellie found that hard to imagine. Whenever they saw Tanty in her fields, she looked hunched over and very, very old.

Tanty lived down the road, on a small farm next to theirs. Ellie didn't know her proper name. Even though they were neighbours, they didn't see her often – except sometimes at the shop, when Mum would say hello to her.

Ellie was worried. "But the other kids say she's a witch."

"Ah well," replied their father, smiling, "and maybe she is, too. Though not all witches are bad, you know."

"You're teasing now," said Ellie.

"Well, maybe just a little. I remember one time," continued Dad, "when my dog had got stuck down a rabbit hole. Tanty knew exactly what to do. She knows about all sorts of things."

"How did she get the dog out of the rabbit hole?" asked Jay.

"Ha!" Dad laughed again. "She grabbed his tail and pulled."

He got up and went over to the sink to wash his hands. "I'm going back out to that fence now. Will you two be all right?"

"Course," muttered Jay.

The twins waited until they heard their father pulling on his boots outside and opening and closing the side gate.

"Old Tanty is crazy," Jay burst out. "She chased Tara and Dave down the road with a big stick!"

"Yes, but they *were* trying to steal her apples," said Ellie.

"So?" huffed Jay. "She's still a crazy old lady.

What about that time she was shouting at Peter?"

Ellie scratched the lamb's head. It looked up at her with bright brown eyes. "Well, maybe she didn't like Peter riding his motorbike around her bottom field."

"And look at her house," continued Jay. "That's a witch's house if ever I saw one."

Ellie had to admit he was right about that. Old Tanty's house was covered in vines and the front yard was full of gnarly trees that looked like goblins.

"Okay, yeah, it *is* kind of scary looking."

"*And* she's got a big black cat," added Jay. "Everybody knows witches have black cats."

"So? We've got a cat," said Ellie, frowning.

"But it's not black. And we don't talk to it like Old Tanty talks to hers. I've heard her. She talks to it like it's a real person."

"Well, at least it doesn't talk back," said Ellie, batting Jay's arm. "Anyway, what if Dad's right? What if Old Tanty *could* help us?

She's so old, maybe she knows about Cloud Riders. I think we should go and ask her."

Jay was silent, but Ellie could tell he was thinking about it. She stood up. "Come on," she said, not really feeling brave at all. "She won't bite."

Chapter 7

OLD TANTY

Old Tanty's house was about ten minutes' walk down the road. Years ago, Mum once told them, Old Tanty and her family had farmed pigs. But her children were grown up now and had gone to live in the city.

The twins stood on the road outside. You could barely see the house from there. The place looked even more overgrown than usual. The gravel driveway was full of puddles, and the letterbox leaned over like a broken tree.

"She's probably out," muttered Jay.

"Look," said Ellie. "There's smoke coming out of the chimney." She set off up the driveway, with Jay following behind. A door at the side of the house was open. On the step sat a big black cat, staring at them. It really did look like a witch's cat.

"That cat doesn't look very friendly," muttered Jay, hanging back.

The cat blinked at them. Then it turned, stood up and walked into the house.

"We should knock," whispered Ellie.

"What're you whispering for?" said Jay loudly.

"I'm not."

"Yes, you are."

A figure appeared in the doorway. "Children," said a cracked voice. It was Old Tanty, with the black cat at her heels. "Have you come to see me?"

"Um, yes," said Ellie nervously. "I hope we're not disturbing you."

"Not at all. Do come in," said the old woman, smoothing down her silvery hair. "I like visitors."

With a gulp, the twins stepped into the house.

"I don't get many visitors, you know," said the old woman, smiling. She reminded Ellie of their grandmother who lived in town, and she relaxed a little.

Inside, the house didn't seem as bad as it did from the outside. There was a cosy fire burning and the walls were covered with pictures. Pictures of pigs, Ellie noticed, looking around. Funny to think that they'd never been inside Old Tanty's house before. It wasn't so different from their own kitchen.

"Have a seat," said the old woman. She was taking piles of newspapers off two chairs near the fire. "Would you like some tea?"

"No, thanks," said Jay, at the same time as Ellie said, "Yes, please."

The old woman hobbled over to the kitchen bench. The twins sat nervously while she put on the kettle. There was a plate of scones on the table, as if she had been expecting them. Soon they were all eating scones with strawberry jam and drinking cups of milky tea.

"Your father used to come down and help

me with the pigs," Tanty told them. "That was after my last son left home."

From its perch on her lap, the black cat stared out at the twins.

"Do you still have pigs?" asked Ellie politely.

"Oh no," Tanty said. "Too much work. I just have my pictures now." She waved at the framed photographs. "That one's Harold." The twins looked up at a photograph of an enormous white pig. "If I was late with his breakfast in the morning, he used to start grunting for me to hurry up."

Jay was starting to fidget in his chair.

"But you young ones haven't come to talk to me about pigs," said Tanty, looking sharply at Jay.

The twins glanced at each other. "You tell her," said Jay.

"We've found something up in the top field," said Ellie nervously, sure that the old woman was about to laugh at her. "Something

that's got hurt, and we don't know how to help it."

"A sheep?" asked Old Tanty, looking from one to the other.

"A Cloud Rider," said Jay.

"Ah," sighed the old woman. "I remember those creatures."

"You *do*?" exclaimed both twins at once.

"Oh, yes," she said. "The first time I saw one, I thought it was a flying rabbit." Jay sniggered.

"I was very young at the time," continued Tanty. "When I was older – about your age – I used to see them all the time."

"There was more than one?" asked Ellie.

"There were dozens of the things. All summer long. You'd see them flying up and down, taking care of the clouds, or whatever it is they do. I haven't seen them in years. I'm glad to hear they're still around."

"The thing is," said Jay, "there's only one of them now."

Old Tanty looked thoughtful. "Is that so?"

"And there are Werrets," said Ellie.

Tanty looked puzzled. "Werrets?"

"They want to make bad weather."

"Well, that's new," sighed Tanty, stroking the black cat.

"And the Cloud Rider's hurt. We want to help him."

"We don't think he can fight the Werrets all by himself," added Jay, very serious now.

Ellie looked at her brother. He was right – she hadn't thought of that before. Ellie didn't think the Cloud Rider could hold out for much longer by himself.

"Do you know how we can help the Cloud Rider?" asked Jay.

Old Tanty was silent for a few minutes. "Many years ago," she said at last, "the old folks had a trick to make sure they had a good summer."

"What did they do?" asked Ellie.

"They used to throw sky berries up at the

clouds," she said.

"Throw *what*?" asked Jay. The twins had never heard of sky berries before.

"Sky berries," repeated Tanty, nodding wisely.

"But where do we find them?" asked Ellie.

"Well, they are tricksy berries," said Tanty. "Hard to find. But I think you might find them in a place you don't usually go to. You'll know when you find them – they're white. I bet that'll fix those Werrets."

The twins looked at each other. "Could it work?" asked Ellie.

The old woman gave them a wink. "It's worth a try."

She showed them to the door. Outside, it looked as if more rain was on the way. Old Tanty clicked her tongue. "So it's those Werrets, is it, making all this bad weather?"

Jay nodded. "That's what the Cloud Rider says."

"Then, I'll tell you what, you'll want to

throw those berries up as high as you can," said Old Tanty.

"Okay," said Ellie. "We'll try."

"Thanks for your help," said Jay, waving goodbye.

"You're very welcome," said the old woman. "Come back and tell me how you get on."

Chapter 8
SKY BERRIES

All the way home, the twins hunted in the bushes along the side of the road.

"Is this one?" asked Jay, holding up a blackberry.

"Don't be silly," said Ellie. "She said they were white."

"I've never seen any berries that are white."

Ellie hadn't either, but she didn't say so. Maybe it was just an old story. She'd never heard of people throwing berries at the clouds either.

"There's probably no such thing," said Jay, kicking at some gravel.

A farmer they knew drove by on a tractor and the twins waved.

Ellie thought about sky berries. Maybe they grew somewhere high, like up in the top field.

"We should go and look in the top field," said Jay, reading her mind as usual.

The twins stopped in at the house to fetch a bag for the berries. The lamb was dozing in the basket. Peter was at the bench, making himself a sandwich.

"Peter," asked Ellie, "have you ever seen any white berries on the farm?"

"Hm, let me think . . ." He bit into his sandwich. "I've seen white mushrooms – is that any help?"

Jay snorted. "We want berries, not mushrooms."

"Well then, I'd look around the back of the shearing shed," he said with a wink.

The twins looked at each other. Of course! There were vines and rubbish and all sorts of overgrown bushes behind the shearing shed. It was a place the twins never went to, just as Tanty had said.

They ran out the door and across the back field to the shearing shed. Although they searched every bush and vine, they didn't find any with white berries.

"Now what do we do?" asked Jay.

A rumble of thunder made them look up. The sky was nearly black. Rain couldn't be far away, so the twins turned to walk back to the house for their coats.

"Where else on the farm don't we go?" asked Ellie, thinking hard.

"Um, how about the fort?" It was actually an old tree hut, but they hadn't played there for ages.

A flash of lightning lit up the sky. The twins looked at each other. They had an idea.

"Are you thinking what I'm thinking?" asked Ellie.

Jay nodded – the firewood trees. They grew thickly up beyond the back field.

"But we're not allowed to go there," said Jay. "Especially not in a storm."

Ellie looked at the sky. "I know," she said, frowning.

Last year, some trees had caught fire in a lightning storm. They were so dry, Dad had called the fire brigade to put the fire out, otherwise they would have lost all their firewood. Mum had told them not to play up there any more.

"But look, the lightning's gone now," said Ellie. "Come on, we'll be all right."

They dashed into the house to get their coats.

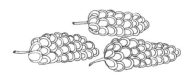

Up among the firewood trees, Ellie and Jay slapped through ferns and low-growing bushes, looking for white berries. Thunder rumbled in the distance.

"Hurry up," said Jay nervously. "I don't want to be in here if there's lightning."

Neither did Ellie. She thought about the lightning striking the trees and setting them alight. Mum would be angry if she knew where they were.

"I can't see any berries," she said.

"Hey!" cried Jay. "I think I've found them."

Ellie hurried over to where Jay was standing next to a large bush. It was covered in white berries. The wind was rising, shaking the berry-laden branches from side to side. Suddenly, there was a crack of lightning and it started to rain.

"Hurry!" shouted Ellie.

Quickly, they pulled off handfuls of berries and put them in their bag. All around them, the trees were creaking in the wind. Ellie looked up fearfully. A flash of lightning lit up the sky and the wind grew even wilder.

"We've got enough!" cried Ellie. "Let's go!"

With a loud snap, a heavy branch broke off a nearby tree. It crashed down onto the bush of white berries, just missing the twins.

Ellie jumped back in fright.

"Run! Head for the cave!" shouted Jay.

When the twins burst into the cave, they couldn't wait to tell the Cloud Rider about the berries – but it was empty.

"Where's he gone?" cried Jay.

"He can't have gone far," said Ellie. But she was worried. What if he had flown away? Perhaps they would never see him again.

They went back outside, into the rain, wondering what to do next. A rustling sound made them look up. The Cloud Rider was sitting up in a tree, head bent under the downpour. His long white feathers were soaked and dripping.

"Can you fly again?" asked Ellie.

"Yes, but not very well. I got caught in this tree."

Jay climbed up to help the creature down from the tree. The Cloud Rider obviously wasn't used to climbing trees. His long legs kept getting tangled in the branches. Jay had to hang on to the creature to stop him from falling. Ellie hurried to help him reach the ground.

"Are you all right?" she asked when he was on the ground at last.

"I am feeling much stronger," he said, ruffling his wet feathers. "Thanks to your help." Even in the rain, he seemed to glow.

"It was the cookie that did it, I bet," said Jay.

The Cloud Rider nodded. "It *was* delicious. Where do they grow?"

The twins burst out laughing, but, though the Cloud Rider looked puzzled, they didn't try to explain why. Telling him how choc-mint cookies were made would be far too hard.

Once they were out of the rain in the cave, Ellie showed him the bag of berries. "We might have found a way to get rid of the Werrets," she said.

The Cloud Rider listened with interest as she explained how they could throw the berries into the clouds.

"Maybe *you* could fly up and throw them?" suggested Jay.

The creature looked sad. "Yes," he said. "But first I must be stronger. I need to be able to fly again. It is still hard for me to lift off from the ground. I must practise more flying before I can risk meeting the Werrets."

The twins decided they would have to come back again the next day. So they left the berries in the cave and ran back home through the rain.

Chapter 9

TAKING FLIGHT

Ellie woke up the next morning feeling excited. She was looking forward to seeing the Cloud Rider flying again. It was still early and she was first in the kitchen. There she saw something amazing. The lamb was out of the basket and taking its first steps.

"You clever thing," she said, kneeling on the floor.

The lamb tottered towards her on its thin, shaky legs. And then, with a little bleat, it collapsed in a heap. Ellie laughed. She picked it up and put it back in the basket.

"What's up?" asked Jay, coming in.

"The lamb's just walked," said Ellie.

Jay went over to the basket. "Not long now," he told it, "and you'll be running around with the other lambs."

Outside, the day was fine, though cloudy. When the twins got to the cave, they found the Cloud Rider sitting on a rock, moving his arms up and down.

"Can you fly today?" asked Jay eagerly.

"Yes, it is possible," said the creature. "I have been practising. I was running up and down the grathe."

"The grass," corrected Jay.

Ellie hid a smile behind her hand. She would have liked to see the creature running up and down the field, flapping his arms.

"But I still cannot get off the ground. I need a high place to jump off."

"The Peak!" said the twins at the same time.

Jay fetched the bag of berries from the cave and they started up the path towards the top field. The Cloud Rider followed behind more slowly. Looking back, Ellie wondered if he was strong enough yet to try proper flying. He looked awfully weak. She shivered.

He would be an easy target if the Werrets attacked again.

At the top field, they stood looking around. The sky was heavy with dark cloud, but there were no Werrets in sight. Perhaps they had gone away?

"Look at all this cloud," sighed the creature. "I will have a lot of work to do."

They went across the field to where a rocky path led up to the top of the Peak. The twins climbed ahead while the Cloud Rider fluttered behind.

As the Cloud Rider stood on a high rock overlooking the top field, the wind ruffled and shivered through his feathers.

Ellie and Jay crouched on rocks behind him, watching. Ellie was holding her breath. Jay had his fingers crossed. Ellie knew exactly what he was thinking. What if the Cloud Rider jumped off and couldn't fly? It was a long drop to the ground below.

The Cloud Rider lifted his arms. Then, suddenly, he jumped.

Ellie gasped. He seemed to be falling, but very slowly. Then a gust of wind picked him up, and the Cloud Rider started to rise. Higher and higher.

Jay was grinning. They watched as the creature lifted on the wind. He looked like a bird, hanging in the air. Then he swooped away, up into the thick clouds, and vanished.

"Where's he gone?" asked Ellie.

The twins stared at the clouds, but the creature was nowhere to be seen. They waited and waited.

"What if he doesn't come back?" said Jay.

"He's got to come back," said Ellie. "For the sky berries." Though she didn't feel so sure.

Jay was silent. She could tell what he was thinking – the Werrets would get the Cloud Rider while he was still weak. Ellie huddled miserably on the rock. They should have waited until he was stronger.

They were still staring at the heavy clouds when they saw an amazing sight. Like a white arrow, the Cloud Rider suddenly shot out of the clouds. The twins jumped to their feet, clapping, as the Cloud Rider swooped down to land in front of them. He had a big smile on his face.

"Now we can scatter your berries," he said.

Jay held out the bag. "Here you are."

The Cloud Rider shook his head. "You can do it," he said.

"What do you mean?" asked Ellie.

"You will fly, too," he said, crouching down. "Climb on my back."

"But we'll be too heavy," protested Ellie. She remembered how light and bird-like he had been when they picked him up. How could he be strong enough to carry both of them?

Jay had no such worries. "Come on," he said to Ellie, looking excited.

The twins hung on to the Cloud Rider's

shoulders. With a lurch, the creature leaped into the air. He was stronger than he looked. Slowly, they rose up into the sky.

"Oh," cried Ellie, thrilled. It was like being on the roller coaster they'd ridden in the city.

Higher and higher they went, up towards the clouds. Far below was their farm, and all the other farms around theirs. The countryside was spread out like a tablecloth. The twins had been in a plane before, but this was completely different.

"Look," cried Jay, "there's our hay barn!"

The Cloud Rider flew easily through the air. He seemed happy to be flying again. He stretched out his arms and they glided along. A bird, flying past, squawked with fright.

A cool wind ruffled Ellie's hair and she laughed out loud. It was incredible. They were flying just below the clouds, high above the green countryside. She saw a truck going along the road. It looked like a toy.

"There's our school," she cried. The

swimming pool was painted bright blue.

Then they turned and headed up through the clouds.

"The berries," cried Jay.

In the excitement of flying, Ellie had forgotten all about them. Hanging on to the Cloud Rider with one arm, Ellie opened the bag with her other hand. The twins took handfuls of berries in their free hands and threw them as high as they could, into the clouds. Would it work?

Chapter 10
THE WERRETS ARE COMING

It was cold up in the clouds and their faces were soon damp with moisture. The clouds were so thick it was like being in fog.

"We shall return now," said the Cloud Rider over his shoulder when they had scattered all the berries.

Ellie was just thinking how relieved she was to be heading back to land when she heard a screech. "What was that?" she asked.

"I don't know," said Jay. He looked worried.

They clung on tighter to the Cloud Rider.

He turned his head and told them, "Do not be afraid, but the Werrets are coming."

The twins looked at each other, sensing each other's fear. Would they get back to the ground again before the Werrets caught up with them? They were so high up. What if the Cloud Rider was attacked and the twins fell off? They wouldn't stand a chance.

Suddenly, out of the clouds, three red shapes appeared. They zapped past the Cloud Rider. Ellie cried out as she felt a blast of heat. The berries – they couldn't have worked!

"Hang on," cried Jay.

The Cloud Rider was swooping through the clouds. Over her shoulder, Ellie could see that the Werrets had turned and were flying after them. They were as fast as jets. Soon they would catch up.

Just at that moment, the Cloud Rider dived to one side, and the Werrets flew past in a rush of heat and sound. Ellie caught a glimpse of burning black eyes.

Up ahead was the Peak. The Cloud Rider was making straight for it. Ellie closed her eyes. Behind her she could hear the swish of the chasing Werrets, getting closer and closer.

The Cloud Rider flew up and over the Peak.

"Yee-ha!" shouted Jay in glee and Ellie opened her eyes.

The Werrets were nowhere to be seen! Still, she was terrified. She wanted to get off the roller coaster now!

"Must get to safety," gasped the Cloud Rider. He was breathing hard.

Out of the cloud, the Werrets appeared once more, heading straight for them. Their pointy faces were brown and sleek like a hawk's. Their burning black eyes were fixed on the Cloud Rider. Ellie screamed.

There was a sickening lurch as the Cloud Rider dived through the cloud. They were going down – fast. The field seemed to be flying up to meet them.

"We're gonna crash!" shouted Jay.

Wind rushed past them. Ellie squeezed her eyes shut and felt her stomach drop as she waited for the impact of the hard ground.

Suddenly, the Cloud Rider flattened out, slowing their fall. At the last minute, he put out his arms, and they glided along above the grass.

The creature stuck out his feet. As they hit the ground, he pounded along in a jerky run. At last he pulled to a stop with a jolt and hung his head, breathing hard. The twins slid quickly off his back.

"Look," said the Cloud Rider, between panting breaths. He pointed up at the sky.

Up above them, one of the Werrets that had been chasing them, suddenly stopped in mid-air. There was a flash of white light, a puff of smoke, and the Werret was gone.

"The berries!" gasped Ellie.

Jay was grinning. "They worked."

"I have never seen that before," said the Cloud Rider, still staring at the sky.

They watched as the other two Werrets flew around in circles. They seemed to be confused. Then they turned and raced away into the distance.

The Cloud Rider looked down at the twins. "They have gone," he said.

"Have they really?" asked Jay.

"Yes, I think so. They did not like those berries in the clouds." The Cloud Rider looked more pleased than they had ever seen him. "You have done well, human children."

Ellie blushed. "Thanks," she said with a shy smile. "Though we did have some help."

"What if they come back?" asked Jay.

"They might, but probably not for a while," said the Cloud Rider. "It will give me time to find some others like myself," he added thoughtfully.

The twins exchanged a glance. "But you will come back, won't you?" asked Ellie.

The Cloud Rider knelt in the grass so that he was face to face with the twins. His eyes were very pale. "Oh, yes, I will come back," he said. "But now I must go. There is much work to be done."

"Okay," said Ellie sadly.

"When will we see you again?" asked Jay.

The Cloud Rider seemed to smile. "Just look up and, if I am there, you will see me."

Then he jumped into the air. They watched as he flew in a circle, like a long wisp of smoke. He swooped down low, and they saw his pale eyes and gentle smile for the last time. Soon he was drifting away, up to the clouds.

The twins waved goodbye until they couldn't see him any more. Ellie felt tears pricking at her eyes at the thought they might not see their friend again. Maybe Jay was feeling the same, because he squeezed her hand.

Back home, Mum was in the vegetable garden. "Have a look at this," she said.

It was the lamb, leaping and running around the garden. It looked very pleased with itself. The twins laughed to see it. Even their dog Fluff was watching the lamb with an amused look.

"We'll keep him as a pet, I think," said Mum.

Ellie hugged the lamb. "That is so amazing!"

"Hey, we could call the lamb Cloud," suggested Jay.

Ellie grinned, thinking about the Cloud Rider. "Good idea."

"And how is your fair-weather friend?" asked their mother.

"Oh, Mum, the Cloud Rider has gone," said Ellie. "We might not see him again!"

Their mother smiled. "Ah well, never mind," she said, and went back to her weeding.

Nobody believes us, thought Jay, shaking his head.

"Except Old Tanty," replied Ellie, reading his mind. "She believes us."

Later that day, the twins walked down the road to visit Old Tanty. They took some spinach from the garden for her. Already the sun was shining and the clouds were nearly gone.

The old woman came to the door of her house, the black cat at her heels. She looked happy to see them.

"The sky berries," said Jay, "they worked!"

"We flew on the Cloud Rider's back," said Ellie, "and threw the berries into the clouds."

Tanty smiled. "Well, well," she said. "Then the old stories turned out to be true."

She was very pleased to get the spinach, and put it on the kitchen bench. "I don't get so many vegetables from my garden any more," she said. "My back gets too sore to bend over."

Ellie had a sudden idea. "We can come and help," she said.

"We can come after school and do some weeding," added Jay.

Tanty's eyes lit up. "Would you really? That would be such a big help."

"Well, you helped us," said Ellie stoutly. "And we saved the Cloud Rider."

They said goodbye to Tanty, promising to visit again soon. The black cat, standing at her feet, seemed to give them a wink.

Two months later, the twins were playing up on the top field again. It was a beautiful day. These days they hardly ever got storms or rainy weather. As always, they kept an eye out for the Cloud Rider. Some days they saw him, other days they didn't.

"I wish we could call out to him," said Jay.

"Then we could give him some honey sandwiches."

"Or choc-mint cookies."

"Oh, look!" cried Ellie, pointing.

There, drifting on a bank of cloud, was the Cloud Rider. The twins jumped up and down, waving madly, but the creature didn't seem to see them. Then they saw why. He was busy – playing with two other, smaller Cloud Riders.

"Oh!" gasped Ellie.

"Cool!" said Jay.

As they watched, the three Cloud Riders sailed off around the Peak and vanished into the clouds.